To Angie, Keeley, and K

Written by Dr. Erica Skidmore & Rev. Ben Skidmore
Illustrations by Kelly Hesson

 / 2000

First Edition

For Jack and Dylan
- E. S. & B. S.

For Mom, Dad, Tracy, and Eric
- K. H.

A Bed for the King

© 2014 On Purpose Press

Text copyright © 2014 Erica Skidmore and Benjamin Skidmore

Illustrations copyright © 2014 Kelly Hesson

All rights reserved. Printed in the United States of America.

ISBN: 978-0-9909633-0-1

First Hardcover Edition (2014)

www.onpurposepress.com

A Bed for the KING

Two birds flew into the barn tweeting excitedly: "The king is coming! The king is coming!"

The king is coming here? The animals were amazed.

They knew they had to prepare something special for the king's visit.

Sheep was sweet and gentle.

"Everyone knows kings like royal things," Sheep said. "I will take my wool to make a rich, fine robe for the king."

When Sheep arrived at the weaver's with her wool, she noticed a little boy in a thin, worn coat sitting outside the door.

He shivered in the cold.

Sheep was moved with compassion. She told the weaver, "Please make a thick, soft blanket and a nice warm coat from my wool."

"Here, child," said Sheep, giving the blanket and coat to the little boy.

"I don't have anything to give you in return," said the boy, "but you can take my old coat."

Sheep didn't know what to do with a tattered coat, but she felt joy in her heart knowing she had done a KINDNESS for a little boy in need.

Ox was big and strong.

There was a man nearby who would pay gold coins to any animal that helped him pull very heavy loads.

"Everyone knows kings like gold," Ox said. "If I work hard, I can get a big stack of gold coins to give to the king."

While he was traveling to visit the man who paid gold coins, Ox passed a field where a farmer was struggling to move a massive boulder.

The farmer was using a shovel and a rope, but he was not strong enough to dig it out alone.

"Maybe I can help," said Ox. He tied the rope around his shoulders. He pulled and pulled and pulled. It took all day, but finally Ox and the farmer moved the rock out of the field.

Ox knew it was too late to go work for the gold coins.

"I don't have any gold," said the farmer.

"But I can give you two bundles of soft, clean hay to thank you for the KINDNESS you've shown me."

Ox felt joy in his heart when he saw how happy the farmer was.

Donkey was thoughtful and creative.

"Everyone knows kings like fancy things," Donkey said. "He will want a grand bed to sleep in."
So Donkey set off to the woodworker's shop with his cart to carry back a fancy bed.

Along the way, Donkey saw a family whose cart had broken down. Donkey knew that he
wouldn't be able to carry a grand bed without his cart, but the family really needed to take
their vegetables to the market.

Donkey stopped. "Please, take my cart to the market," he said to the family.

"We don't have money to pay you," said the mother.

"But here, let me make you something you can use," said the father. He took boards from his broken wagon and made a feeding box, called a manger, for Donkey to take back to the barn.

It wasn't a fancy bed, but Donkey headed home feeling joy in his heart, knowing he had done a KINDNESS for someone in need.

Donkey, Ox, and Sheep all arrived back at the barn late that evening.
None of them had gotten the gifts they had wanted.
Donkey put his manger down in the middle of the barn, and Ox placed his clean,
soft hay inside. Finally, Sheep placed her tiny cloth coat on top of the hay.

"This isn't a good present for a king," said Donkey.

"What will we do now?" wondered Sheep.

Just then, the innkeeper brought a man and a woman into the barn. "I'm sorry there aren't any open rooms," said the innkeeper. "Since you are going to have a baby *very* soon, though, you can stay in the barn. You will be warm, safe, and dry in here."

Later that night, the woman gave birth to a baby boy. She wrapped him in the cloth Sheep had brought.

Then she placed the tiny bundle into the manger filled with soft hay.

The woman smiled gently at the animals, "Thank you so much!" she told them.

"This is everything I needed for my baby." The animals felt joy in their hearts.

Soon important people arrived from far away. They had come to visit the new baby.

"Friends," Ox said to Donkey and Sheep, "This little baby is the King we have been waiting for!"

Even though they didn't get a royal robe, gold coins, or a fancy bed, the animals all did a KINDNESS for those who needed help. And their KINDNESS made a perfect bed for the King.

Sheep, Ox, and Donkey used what they had to do a KINDNESS for others. By doing a KINDNESS, they helped make a bed for the King.

As you prepare for Christmas, create a new, soft bed for the King. Celebrate every KINDNESS you do by placing a hay ribbon in the manger as a reminder.

May you feel God's joy in your heart as you prepare a Bed for the King this year!